RETROSPECTIVE

A POETRY COLLECTION

BY KELLY VAN NELSON

MMH PRESS

Copyright © Kelly Van Nelson
First published in Australia in 2021
by MMH Press
Waikiki, WA 6169

All Rights Reserved. No part of this book may be used or reproduced by any means, graphic, electronic, or mechanical, including photocopying, recording, taping or by any information storage retrieval system without the written permission of the copyright owner except in the case of brief quotations embodied in critical articles and reviews.

Because of the dynamic nature of the Internet, any web addresses or links contained in this book may have changed since publication and may no longer be vaild. The views expressed in this work are solely those of the author and do not necessarily reflect the views of the publisher and the publisher hereby disclaims any responsibility for them.

 A catalogue record for this work is available from the National Library of Australia

National Library of Australia Catalogue-in-Publication data:
Retrospective/Kelly Van Nelson

ISBN: 978-0-6451483-0-5
(Hardback)

ISBN: 978-0-6450966-3-7
(Paperback)

ISBN: 978-0-6450966-4-4
(eBook)

PRAISE FOR THE AUTHOR

This collection has a timeless message that lends itself to the current generation … painting a picture of a fierce warrior who is both strong and protective, an advocate of fairness when there's none, and a multi-coloured messenger of truth and hope worthy of any urban wall.

Dannielle Line, Author and Editor

Kelly Van Nelson's website is titled with the description: EDGY STORIES FROM INSIDE THE MIND. I find this an apt description of her poetry. It's very edgy, an unfiltered musing on the darker elements present within society. The hidden, the insidious, the things people want to hide from. Her prose is powerful, and rather impressive. Kelly Van Nelson is a talent to watch, and for those interested in the Australian poetry scene.

Theresa Smith Writes

This book is packed with heavy themes and raw, unfiltered poetry that speaks directly to the poet's experience of violence, abuse, and bullying. The author's working-class upbringing informs her perspective, lingering in the corners of most poems, sometimes with nostalgia and sometimes with powerful, bitter resonance.

Holden Sheppard, Author

This poet's work began with themes gathered in her early days as an underdog on a council estate in Newcastle-Upon-Tyne. Using simple powerful language, she offers the reader a very personal perspective about life on the gritty side. With honesty and heart, Van Nelson tackles concerns such as discrimination, corporate and playground bullying, domestic violence, mental illness, and other important social justice issues. This collection speaks of hard yards and heartbreak, but there is also a sense of hope and courage.

Writing WA

To keep your truth in sight you must keep yourself in sight and the world should be a mirror to reflect your image and to reflect upon. This is exactly what Kelly Van Nelson conveys. It is her journey, the good the bad and the ugly. By putting it to paper she turns her experiences into a way to bounce back from her underdog world and help others in the process. We are thrilled to have her collection of poetry in our Hollywood Swag Bags honouring Oscar Weekend.

Lisa Gal Bianchi

The beauty of poetry, when it is written exceptionally well takes you to a place of vulnerability. It gets your heart beating and your thoughts branching out to question, to wonder, to connect, to understand, to break the barriers of judgment. Kelly Van Nelson is one such poet that takes you one step further than this, diving into a world that hits so many relevant topics in today's world. It's not just poetry. It's hard core magic. This masterpiece touched my soul.

Micky Martin, Author

Graffiti Lane swaps rose-coloured glasses for grit, dirt, and shadow. There's a rawness and simplicity to the language that evokes feelings of empathy, "I've-been-there" understanding, empowerment, sadness, tenderness and even smiles. One minute you're wincing and the next you're nodding your head – it's that kind of poetry; poetry that gets people, that reveals the poet's heart, poetry that packs a punch.

Monique Mulligan, Author

Poetically written, the rawness of the words immediately drew me in from the first page. Written in an utterly honest fashion, Kelly Van Nelson skilfully explores both the darker side of human nature, as well as the hope and resilience within every one of us. Profoundly moving and emotionally charged, I loved reading it.

Yu Dan Shi, Author of Come Alive

Great collection of poems showcasing deep insight into the human psyche as it deals with life's challenges. The author has a natural talent of capturing the raw feelings and artistically playing it back in beautiful language. Highly recommended for anyone interested in diving into life's emotional roller coaster.

Omar Alim

A well-written and thought-provoking book of poetry that leaves the reader reflecting on the emotional intensity of the words and message relayed through them. Highly recommended.

Danielle Aitken, Author

This collection of urban poetry is just incredible. Sometimes challenging to read, because of the emotions it invokes or the fact you think on it for a while. Some beautiful moments too. The author has an incredible voice and her works in this book have something for everyone.

Jacie Anderson, Author

Dark and distressing themes are laid bare, yet accomplished poet Kelly Van Nelson manages to imbue a sense of hope, rather than hopelessness, approaching every topic with unwavering honesty, unafraid to venture into harrowing territory to reflect on a myriad of challenges. Using the vernacular of the street, the boardroom and the domestic front, Van Nelson reveals a keen sensory perceptiveness, an acute awareness of injustice, a deep-rooted empathy, and the life-altering potential of resilience.

Maureen Eppen, Author and Blogger

This collection provides a raw, eclectic mix of poems relating to many of today's issues. What I liked most about it is the accessibility of the writing, which is understandable and highly emotive.

Lisa Wolstenholme, Author

Graffiti Lane is an engaging collection of poems that revolve around the concept of being the underdog, bullying and finding ways to bounce back. The poet's angst and fear will help readers perceive the broader effects of discrimination and bullying as they bleed into teenage bullying, corporate bullying and harassment, gender inequality, domestic violence, and suicide. The poems are raw, dark, and intense and will take readers to a dimension where they realize that there is always hope.

Mamta Madhavan for Readers' Favourite

Punch and Judy explores the horrors of relationship breakdown in graphic detail, yet, for me, anyway, it was not so much a horror story as one of growth and resilience. Even in her darkest moments, 'Judy' asserts her right to be; she is an everywoman, a heroine who we feel deeply for, willing her on and applauding her efforts to extricate herself from the toxicity in which she finds herself enmired. A rollicking tale in verse, with an economy of words that really pack a punch with every line. Make yourself a big pot of coffee, sit down and enjoy the ride!

Julia Kaylock, poet

What a ride Rolling in the Mud is, from the sly humour of a cheeky widower getting pay back to the desperation of bullying and abuse, this collection takes you through the gamut of emotions. I had intended to pace myself and read just a couple of stories at a time and instead found myself reading it all in one day. Thoroughly enjoyed it and well recommended.

Karyl Treble

Punch and Judy is an expressive, hard hitting, and intense form of contemporary poetry from Kelly Van Nelson. Although deeply serious in tone, this is a creative and theatrical collection that will draw in both fans of the poetry field and new readers to this emotive form of writing. It is clear Kelly Van Nelson is quite the figurehead in terms of contemporary Australian poetry. Her writing is powerful, moody, targeted, and emotive. Every word has been carefully selected and each separate poem thoughtfully produced. In this world of increasing domestic violence, continual images of toxic relationship breakdowns, unacceptable attitudes in relation to sexism and negative behaviours, it is high time a progressive collection such as Punch and Judy is released in public sphere. Keynote literature such as Punch and Judy can help lead the way in terms of breaking down barriers and can work to change public perceptions with regards to relationship challenges.

Amanda Barrett, Mrs B's Book Reviews

Also by Kelly Van Nelson

POETRY

Graffiti Lane
(MMH Press 2019)

Punch and Judy
(MMH Press 2020)

Graffiti Lane Collector's Edition
(MMH Press 2020)

LITERARY FICTION

Rolling in the Mud
(Ginninderra Press 2020)

The Pinstripe Prisoner
(Serenity Press 2021)

RETROSPECTIVE

To my forever friends
Angela Evans and Emma Bailey

when I look back
you are always there
sharing laughter and tears
as we spin on life's dancefloor

RETROSPECTIVE

"thinking about or connected with something that happened in the past."

OXFORD ENGLISH DICTIONARY

*"One day, in retrospect,
the years of struggle will strike you
as the most beautiful."*

SIGMUND FREUD

FOREWORD

FOREWORD FROM THE AUTHOR

Growing up in Newcastle-upon-Tyne was rough. Not because I lived in an inner-city council estate, ranked in the bottom 5% of deprived areas in the UK. That was just bricks and mortar. But because inside those four walls there was no love to be found. Only cracks hidden beneath woodchip paper. I used to lie in the top bunkbed in a tiny room I shared with my sister, picking those little chips out of the wallpaper at night, splinters getting stuck under my nails as I tried to ignore the arguments going on downstairs.

At school, I had a close bunch of friends, many of whom are still by my side today, sharing the laughter and the tears from wherever we are in the world. We are connected by the strongest bond of our youth, unbreakable by the vast distance between us or the time that ticks by in the blink of an eye. The truly special people in life are the ones who lighten the load for others, and I share this book with those who took the heavy lifting out of my baggage, especially during my younger turbulent years.

Then there was the other bunch who called names, spread toxic hatred, taunted, tormented, and bullied. We too are connected by the steely strength I found in rising above their relentless efforts to bring down a lost girl who was attempting to blend in with the classroom crowd, desperately trying to be the same as everyone else and failing.

> I was never meant
> to be the same
> as everyone else –
> I know that now.

I'm proud that I left school at sixteen and carved a new path for myself, trailblazing my way to kick new goals with an unlimited supply of blood, sweat and tears as fuel. My upbringing and turbulent high school days gave me the mental strength to achieve anything. As such, I've taken creative liberties with the genius of Pink Floyd in asking our teachers to look out for those kids in the class who aspire to be so much more than the label of their circumstances and for society to judge just a little bit less the teens who leave the system too soon.

Being uneducated past high school, but with a bucketload of experience on my resume on how to overcome the grittiest challenges, is what made me who I am today. Someone who will hold out a hand for the underdog, not to prop them up, but to guide them on their own journey towards wherever they want to go. The business leader who values honest relationships and an ethical team above all else. The poet who speaks out to make the world a better place. The mum and the wife, juggling life's crazy schedule with constant gratitude and a healthy dose of passion.

This book stems from the many snippets I have stored away in the back of my mind of growing up. I have no photographs of childhood before my teenage years, so these poems are constructed from my interpretation of the past from hazy recollections of life in Newcastle-upon-Tyne as an eighties child. During the process of writing this manuscript I unearthed many tough memories that have been buried away for years. What I do know is music was consistently my saviour and the colourful nightclubs of the North East were my escape. My father, who passed away in his forties, was impartial to Whitesnake and would blare *'Ain't No Love in the Heart of the City'* at every opportunity. My mother had posters of Guns N' Roses, Springsteen, and Bon Jovi hanging all over the walls of our home. Many musical references, not just Pink Floyd, are weaved through these poems in tribute to this era. I have taken creative liberties with these rock and pop threads and with my retrospective memories. I'm a terrible singer, but this book is my tune, beat, rhythm and soul, played on the ghetto blaster of many open mics and slams around the world where I have vocalised several of these poems in spoken word form.

Thank you for picking up a copy of 'Retrospective' and pressing play. I hope by the last page you either love it so much you loan it to your friend and drop a book review into the public domain, or at the very least feel compelled to press rewind on the boombox to go at it again, for I believe wholeheartedly in giving people a second chance.

Kelly
xxx

CONTENTS

ANOTHER BRICK 1
NOSTALGIA 3
BLUE BLOOD.. 4
CABBAGE PATCH KID (REWIND) 7
LOYALIST ROYALIST 8
RHUBARB AND CUSTARD... 10
ALTERNATIVE CONSERVATIVE 11
DEAR SANTA.. 12
SWEET SHOP 14
GUNS N ROSES 15
VELVET CURTAINS 16
CHIP ON MY SHOULDER 18
UNCLE SAM 19
BLASTAWAY... 21
PAC-MAN.. 22
CIAO BABY 23
TEACHER'S PET 25
MIA MAMA... 27
WHEN WILL I BE FAMOUS? 28
BREAKING THE RULES 29
SHE WOLF.. 32
MILK BOTTLES 33
FORK... 36
MIME... 37
BLACKBOARD 38
MACK THE KNIFE 39
BOOMBOX.. 40
HAIRSPRAY.. 41
ANOTHER BRICK 42
IT JUST IS 44
HOME COOKED GRATITUDE... 47

AIN'T NO LOVE	**49**
INTERVIEW WITH A VAMPIRE GIRL	51
3AM CINCUAIN	52
DANCE	53
DISCO BALL	54
FLUORESCENT ADOLESCENT	54
AIN'T NO LOVE	55
INVISIBLE THREAT	56
CHARLIE	57
THE HOPPINGS	58
BINGO	59
HAIR OF THE DOG	60
N-TRANCE	61
YO-YO	62
CATPHISH	63
DIRTY MIND	66
SNAKEBITE	67
JAM AND SPOON	67
RAPUNZEL	68
HOLLOW	69
ASH	70
EXPLOSIVE CALAMITY	71
AI	73
CALCULATED RISK	74
LIT	75
NIGHT IN	76
APPRECIATED	77
COAT HANGER	78
OUTBREAK	79
LEV-I	80
RED HAND GANG	81
LOVE IS A BATTLEFIELD	83
PINK LANE	84
BOYS DON'T CRY	85
ROAD	86
OMITTED PUNCTUATION	87

SIMPLE MATH 88
CUBE (REWIND) 89
HEART 92
DON'T LOOK BACK **93**
BIG COUNTRY 95
DECEASED ESTATE 96
DON'T PREACH 97
PLANET EARTH 98
ACE OF SPADES 99
POP CULTURE 100
EYES IN THE BACK OF MY HEAD 101
BELLYBUTTON OF THE UNDERBELLY 102
STEEL HEART 105
ALWAYS SPACE 105
CATCH MY BREATH 106
BORDER CONTROL 106
FUTURE PROOF 107
SHADOW 108
GEORDIE SHORE 109
THE CURE 110
MAKE HAY 111
TEEN ADVICE 112
IMPOSTER SYNDROME 113
DETENTION 114
NEOTERIC DIMENSION (REWIND) 115
ODE TO RESILIENCE 116
RED LIGHT 117
HOT WHEELS 119
ROCK PAPER SCISSORS 120
NO PLACE CALLED HOME 123
TRIBE 125
SONGBIRD 126
PICK UP STICKS 127
COALITION 129
WALLFLOWER AWAKENING 130
THE EDGE 132

MASTERCHEF	133
WAY BACK WHEN	134
A TRIBUTE TO BILLY ELLIOT	135
GOODBYE, PET	136
PLEASURE DOME	137
MUTATE	138
DON'T LOOK BACK (REWIND)	139
THIS IS MY AXIS	141
WEATHER GIRLS	142
GROUND ZERO	144
L PLATES	145
TOBY JUG	146
FEAR	147
BRIDGE OVER TROUBLED WATER	148
DARK SIDE OF THE MOON	150
PERSPECTIVE	151
ACKNOWLEDGEMENTS	**153**
ABOUT THE AUTHOR	**157**

ANOTHER BRICK

NOSTALGIA

I crossed the Tyne Bridge out of Newcastle
And the Sydney Harbour Bridge into New South Wales
Structures designed by one architect
Built by the same contractor
My bridges over troubled water
I look back in retrospection with nostalgia.

BLUE BLOOD

Dragged up on an estate
decorated with public housing warning,
none of its residents would receive a calling
to progress through school with acclaimed graduation
of a pathway to higher exams to shower in affirmation,
washing sweatbox skin into a lather of self-worth
in the name of an education truly worthy
of pinning to the front of an ancient fridge
with a magnet from the cereal box
for Papa to admire when he went in search
of a cold brandless beer
except Papa was upstairs
trying to climb over the pearly gates
locked to him for eternity
for not getting his daughter into university
before he checked out with an artery bursting in a flood,
staining the ground with
blue working-class blood.

Mama remarried again … and again … and again;
the postman who knocked twice,
a barman pulling pints,
a coward who liked to kick off fights
inside our four walls of shame
surrounding a family with no regal name
to pass down through generations
of red-blooded male masterpieces,
who dress in white collar, or don't even bother
to work when their allowance
puts them safely on the outskirts
of the concrete jungle where the
lion doesn't sleep tonight
as it's always roaring at the door

ready to tear hunks of meat from us girls
to feed insatiable hunger of a loser in the hood
aggrieved at the unfair genetics of
blue working-class blood.

On the other side of the tracks
the silver spoon shines brightly with promise
of a career where I can peel off the blue collar
to put on pinstripe suit and make a decent dollar
way above minimum wage
where the union is filled with outrage
at the injustice of the waste of a girl like me
with the brains to be
so much more than a picket line statistic
lost in a Thatcher pessimistic era
of steel workers cut and coal mines shut
and forgotten girls with potential caught in a rut,
their starved bodies resigned to vice
or me with weary hands stuck in a vice,
having my callused fingers worked to the bone
until they seep and I weep fat drops of
blue working-class blood.

I was sewn up a thousand times
with a needle and thread
leaving a trail of scars from my toes to my head
that was screwed on,
always looking forward and never back
for fear of seeing flashbacks
of flaking scabs from those picket lines
I used to pick off my skin,
leaving nothing but a thin
veil over saddened wise eyes,
witness to so much poverty
and humanitarian demise
of blue blood residents stuck on the wrong side

of the tracks, veins now filled with despise
that they couldn't afford a first-class train fare
out of there to revise
their future in a carriage reserved
only for passengers with
red blood.

CABBAGE PATCH KID (REWIND)

It was barren under the Christmas tree
after Papa slammed the door
returning no more to face the awkward silence
following noisy violence
causing post-traumatic stress disorder
lifelong implications from argumentative lacerations
stripping the woodchip wallpaper bare
leaving nothing but paper-thin walls
to offer little protection from me listening in despair
from beneath the tent of my duvet.

All I wanted was a hug of free love
and a Cabbage Patch Doll
that was all the rage amongst friends
for me to adore with all her imperfections
drowning in those big eyes that had seen too much
admiring podgy cheeks
that fooled the world into thinking
her soul was well nourished.

Papa said left
Mama said right
my young veins bled every word of their fight
I heard him say with outrage
the doll was delivered in the mail
Mama said he lied
Papa broke down and cried
accusing her of taking it back to the store
for rum and black money.

Only the Cabbage Patch Kid
knows the truth
of my youth.

REWIND - Cabbage Patch Kid was first published in Full House Magazine, 2021.

LOYALIST ROYALIST

Nose pressed against dirty window,
eyes wide, watching the bustle
as they set up trestle tables
opposite the house on the crescent
of green grass marring the concrete,
a token gesture planted by the council
to remind us we are not
the forgotten generation.

Mismatched seats dragged
from every roughcast property,
laid in perfectly uniformed
compulsive disorder lines,
positioned within easy reach
of the egg sandwich platters
put out by the next-door neighbour
who went above and beyond,
cutting the crusts off and sculpting
the white bread in neat shapes
that match the triangular bunting
of union jacks airing their importance
in the breeze, knowing with certainty
they are way more than the bee's knees,

                                        "God Save the Queen".

My best skirt has an oil stain on the front
from playing amongst ancient tools in the garden shed.

Panicked fingers claw at my head
still itchy from the trauma of last month's nits,
afraid my sister left behind an egg
in her daily pickings and it's hatched.

She looks posh in her Sunday oversized dress,
one size too big so she has room to grow into it –
hope she looks after it so when it passes down to me

it doesn't have oil stains on it too – Keep it clean!
                              "God Save the Queen".

Take a deep breath and get ready
to be marched over the road
by Mama in her high heels and plum lipstick.

Older boy from five doors down
takes pride of place at the top of the table,
my sometimes friend sits at his princely side,
white veil over smug face
far removed from Diana's grace.

My blue eyes sting as I hold back young tears,
cheeks red from anger and shame,
I will never be good enough to play
Lady Diana on her wedding day.

I didn't want to go
but was forbidden to be a no show,
Loyalist Royalists,
we all have to bow,
because this is the only thing to happen in this street
that doesn't involve a police intervention
handcuffing the red, white, and blue dream,
                              "God Save the Queen".

RHUBARB AND CUSTARD

Rhubarb grew in wild bunches
in the back garden
behind the rabbit shed

Mama called it a weed
with poisonous raw stalks
never to be touched

We were served a treat
of the sweet tinned variety
in a pool of custard from a carton

I never strayed
to the forbidden weed –
well, not that kind anyway

Only in my adult years
did the forbidden fruit
become my favourite dessert

ALTERNATIVE CONSERVATIVE

Baroness Iron lady,
three terms undefeated
all in her stride,
confident or conceited?

Political coups
in financial deregulation,
flexible labour, puppetry unions,
an era of privatisation.

Chopped at the knees
following strikes and poll tax,
yet an icon for strong women
despite succumbing to the axe.

DEAR SANTA

All I want for Christmas, Mama,
is a friend called Ken who is not imaginary
and a doll called Barbie
with hair so clean it must surely be washed
more often than just on Sundays
and so many clothes they would not come close
to fitting in the miniscule cupboard
I share with my sister.

All I want for Christmas, Mama,
is a teddy with fur so soft it can soak up my tears
while I cuddle it and whisper goodnight
and a permanently podgy stomach
because this bear is lucky enough to
know what it's like to feel full inside.

All I want for Christmas, Mama,
is a chocolate box filled with treats
in colourful wrappers still good enough to eat
instead of gooey and congealed to the paper,
their Velcro a mottled grey coating
from weariness at being re-gifted
way too long after the use by date.

All I want for Christmas, Mama,
is a pristine CD
begging to be lifted from the scratched polystyrene box
to be played on my second-hand stereo
instead of the disappointment
of opening a barren case
and being spun a gut-wrenching white lie
about the disc being stolen in the shop
even though my brother has been playing
the compilation for months.

All I want for Christmas, Mama,

is a hug so tight it squeezes
the breath from my bony ribcage
and a kiss on the top of my curly mop
that makes me open my naive arms wide
and my heart wider
because I feel as special
as the Angel of the North.

All I want for Christmas, Mama,
is you,
but I stopped believing
in Santa Clause a long time ago.

SWEET SHOP

Ten pence bonbons in a white paper bag
Twirled at the edges to seal in the goods

Cola bottle fizzers bitter on innocent tongue
Giving sugar rush to young blood

Swizzle stick taking the lick
Doubled dipped in orange and cherry sherbet

Bassett's liquorice allsorts, red shoelace substitutes
Or black and white magpie mint humbugs

Edible love hearts with messages carved in mind for life
Matlow knew exactly how to win a girl over

Corner shop lady who knew you by name
Extinct forever, bulldozed by supermarket chain

Turf wars in a concrete jungle with no turf
Gun fights without expensive bullets only knives
Thorns without roses in the backyard
These were the days of our lives

GUNS N ROSES

Gangs to the north of the Tyne
Throwing rocks to the south of the Quays
Football anthems sung from the terrace
Relegation brought us all to our knees

VELVET CURTAINS

Young feet, blue toes, curled
in unfashionable Derry boots
I hated, out of date fashion statement,
swopped halfway to school for sandals
to avoid the popular girl debasement
because I wanted to fit in,
my sister by my side because Mama
didn't do the ride
to drop us off inside
the gateway to education.

Parent night came
but my parents never came
to hear about my Grade A
so I hung my head in shame
when even the naughtiest kid on the block
had someone there to hear about their claim to fame
as the class idiot.

I was the invisible good girl
who stood on stage in the school play
holding back tears on the day
nobody in the audience came to pay
their respect to my moment in the spotlight
and the pain wouldn't go away
as I searched the clapping crowd again and again
looking for a familiar face of a proud relative
and finding nothing but faceless strangers
looking my way
as I tried to hide the dismay
behind the velvet curtains of an encore.

Great expectations became fiction,
Dickens read to avoid friction
of asking for affection

or daring to hope for the basis of a good recollection
to be formed, that in later years might make
the old days seem not that bad at all,
but that memory never came.

All I have is the same replay
of disappointment
permanently recorded on my brain.

CHIP ON MY SHOULDER

walls
enclose
poverty
woodchip
mocking
me

UNCLE SAM

My teenage body germinating
a coming of age mentality,
sat upright the day the troops stormed class
to recruit all the lads; I was the only lass
who raised a voluntary arm
still numb from the BCG vaccine
regime designed to make sure we were a pristine,
clean, human machine
to be taken away to glean our dreams
and carve core skills to make the next generation
of Privates who could scale military ranks
from frontline trenches to driving tanks.

It was the first time I'd ever seen green
in an otherwise grey world
and I was drawn to the appeal
of stepping into newly camouflaged skin
where I would never be a misfit again;
relishing the idea of modelling a child's uniform
that blended in to be the exactly the same
as every other figure in the frame,
giving adequate protection from the giveaway
of a hole in trainers from the mart
that spelled out the cruel fact
I could never master the art
of looking like a kid born with privilege.

The jabbed bruise on my arm screamed
to be selected for work experience,
desperate to punch higher
than the heavy weight of a weary heart
sparring to have a fighting start in life.

They marched me away for a training day,
to tackle mud run pain with the lure of regular pay
with a compass as my new friend

desperately trying to show the way
to a utopian place where North
had all the magnetic pull on the planet
before my teacher rained on the parade
of the only female applicant
who didn't fit the profile of a regular candidate
proficient in urinal use,
leaving my aspirations wounded,
unable to soldier on.

Taking a bullet isn't fatal
when resilience is made from Kevlar
built up over years of living in the conflict zone
of a broken home
in an inner city prone
to never throwing the dog a bone.

I soldiered on taking a new tact
of building a career down another track
onto the battlefield we all must combat
to infiltrate the employment field.

Over the years the rules of engagement changed
with women beginning to make the grade,
lining up after graduation convocation
to gain the accolade
of fighting for their country
in the desperate quest for equality.

These nieces of Uncle Sam
are in the army now,
even though I
am not.

Instead, I wave my flag at full mast
because the war of these women
making it in a historical man's world
is won.

BLASTAWAY

Shops boarded up, a dilapidated eyesore,
teenagers hovering, nowhere to go,
drinking Castaway mixed with Diamond White
to Blastaway cobwebs and help us fight

… depression.

PAC-MAN

Happiness came in a box
filled with white cheese whatsits
of polystyrene foam
protecting an oversized monitor
and a dot.matrix printer

Every spare minute engrossed
in the cassette ribbon embossed
with a greedy yellow man
waiting to play in the maze
of an arcade game craze

I watched enviously
as he ate power pellets
until his round belly was so full
he could barely move fast enough to escape
four ghosts of colourful evil intent

Mine rumbled in hunger
and I wanted to dive into the screen
to share his meal
but it was not to be

      … the computer says no

CIAO BABY

Wandered around the city today,
shopping bags swinging,
filled with this season's fabric
from the Quayside market,
immaterial lining for a later landfill –
so much to be grateful for.

Saw a church in the distance,
doors open on a Sunday afternoon,
compelled to pop in to untangle words
from silent torment of mundane,
a release of confused letters
encased in sanctuary of mind,
blessed is this mother tongue of mine –
so much to be grateful for
in being able to speak freely.

Eyes adjust to gloom;
ignore the slivers of light
filtering through stained glass,
attention captured instead by the figure
on the alter beneath the cross –
so much to be grateful for,
every unique stranger a miracle,
this angel is bare foot and sleeping.

Lower my head and say a prayer
for the homeless young woman resting
weary head on a supermarket carrier bag –
so much to be grateful for,
the blanketing bed awaiting me at home;
suspect her makeshift pillow
contains fashions of another season.

Sit there long to implore a power
greater than us both for answers –
so much to be grateful for;
it is time to put food in her stomach,
warmer clothes on her back,
a roof over her head
when the church closes for the night.

She stirs as I stand –
so much to be grateful for
as she stretches her arms wide,
embracing everything life has to offer
before rummaging inside her pillowcase
for an old overcoat decorated with holes
as I contemplate the absurdity of my purchases.

So much to be grateful for
as the coins jingle with the church bells as I rummage
further into my purse to find sweet rustle of paper
and press a note into an outstretched palm
before slotting loose change into church collection box;
light a candle burning a flame of hope
as she walks away into the light outside –
ciao baby.

TEACHER'S PET

Education is a dual opportunity

the pearly gate of life
and
the pearly gate of death

because only teacher's pets go to heaven

School is the beginning, middle, and end
of a bedtime story told every night
by an absent mama working three jobs
who never tucks me in
(couldn't, wouldn't, shouldn't)

I pack a Tupperware of best behaviour
next to the dinner ticket
burning a hole through the hand-me-down pocket
as classroom lessons begin
for the kids not truanting –
maybe they want to go to heaven too

Pay attention from the front row
raising hand high to answer questions
indignant when not asked
to contribute to a discussion
about subjects that matter
like Algebra because we all need to know our
(square) roots
to stand a chance of becoming
the teacher's pet

English literature double period
curriculum books galore to absorb
new sentences scrawled on the blackboard
white chalk on black
but can't concentrate after the ruler smack
on the back of my head from the school d**khead

followed by a ruler smack on the back of my hand
from the teacher for not focusing on
the writing on the wall

I'll have to break out of this cage on my own –
Who decided teachers could keep pets anyway?

MIA MAMA

mia
mama
too strict
putting in place
curfew before dark
freedom stripped bare
cut access to phone calls
from boy with ulterior motive
inside/outside half-moon snores
tiptoes avoid creaky floorboards
this girl has never been kissed
a white lie whispered tonight
by who's that girl madonna
bypassing sweet sixteen
papa don't preach
or live to tell
mama
mia

WHEN WILL I BE FAMOUS?

Grolsch bottle tops threaded through lace loops
clicking as we walked the school corridors

Synthetic shell suits in gaudy colours
a fire hazard covering the poverty monkey on our backs

Shoulder pads sharp enough to poke out enemy eyes
as we practiced power stances to build a Dynasty

Bum bags to hold the cash none of us had
close to our lithe bodies

Leg warmers above yellow fluorescent stilettoes
to beat the cold weather north of the wall

Fingerless gloves made of fishnet
worn in the hood by prima donna's

Brosette's with ripped kneecaps
in soft faded denim wondering

… when will I be famous?

BREAKING THE RULES

I broke every rule when I graduated school
at sixteen with certificates filled with GCSE's,
Grade A but still no university degree,
I couldn't afford to pay the fee
when everything I earned from
sweeping floors at the hairdressers,
serving six pack bread buns in the bakers,
flipping burgers wrapped in grease proof paper,
went to paying the council official dividends
courtesy of government lip service assistance
for the four walls of roughcast housing
camouflaged in a concrete jungle;
even the SAS would struggle to rescue
the girl who always knew
life came with a renewed
daily mission.

I broke every rule when I became a mule,
smuggling my under-age innocence
beneath feigned self-confidence
onto the bus to London, down a one-way street
travelling from Newcastle
on a ticket bought without parental guidance
because even though they say
blood is thicker than water
it can also clot the veins
and I wanted to cut the reigns
from my mother and never look back
and papa didn't care since the day
he left me standing alone there
while he rushed upstairs with a burst artery
that flooded his heart with
bleeding instead of beating,
never coming back downstairs again
to see the girl cut off her pigtails

to transform into someone
that dovetails seamlessly into society.

I broke every rule when I kept my cool
because nobody who comes
from a broken home wants to be broken,
so I survived alone in the big smoke
with a few pounds tucked in my coat pocket,
a pocket rocket, spending the rest on night school
to show the world I was no fool,
even though the Queen's English evaded thee
and privilege passed over me
I was damn smart, playing the part,
refining my art, giving myself a kick start,
following premeditated flow chart
into a job answering the phone,
faxing memo, trying to erase the memories
of neglected younger years
and all the deeply rooted fears
that I was never going to be good enough
and imposter syndrome would forever be
my only companion.

I broke every rule not to be cruel
but to be kind to myself
when my boss chose to remind me
that I had made it so far as to fly the cuckoo's nest
and I should never rest
until I succeeded in making the migration
from there to here worthwhile,
never clipping my own frantically flapping wings,
because only you can spread those wings and fly
… so high I could well see papa
and he might just see
the woman I'd grown up to be.

I broke every rule when I put on a dual hat,
corporate executive with a feather in my cap
and a cap in my hand,
working 24/7 building organisational brand
before the darkness sets in
and the side hustle kicks in
as a poet with deeply rooted scars
engrained in a sonnet,
with that feather in cap
overshadowed in mental pain
from the threat of a sting
from the bee in my bonnet,
buzzing so loudly it's a struggle to remember
that I really did cut those pigtails off
and it's time to tell tales
of truth overflowing with what's real,
helping to heal this soul who broke
and was put back together on an open mic
baring every crack in the spotlight,
not caring if this poem is filled
with so many loose threads
it can never be wound on a spool,
because I'm still the goddamn sharpest tool
in the box that you can't box me into,
because I'll always be the girl
who broke every rule in the school
who grew into a woman
who would rather rhyme to make a dime
than recline and decline
back into old skool.

SHE WOLF

spirit
found at sixteen
growing up beyond years
insecure sheep dressed in wolf's clothes
fearless

MILK BOTTLES

There are ten milk bottles standing on the wall
waiting for the milkman to call
and not one of them was emptied by me;
my baby milk was the powdered type
so I never started out life
having a taste for the good stuff.

There are nine milk bottles standing on the wall
waiting for the milkman to call
after he parks on the double yellow
just beyond the gate
and wanders up the garden path
with a spring in his step, whistling Springsteen
as Mama shakes her head and says,
"never trust a man in a big white van",
refusing to let him inside to
pay him in kind.

There are eight milk bottles standing on the wall
waiting for the milkman to call,
although maybe he won't bother showing up today
since Mama refused to flirt with him
and told him the milk was going off,
but she's been letting the postman
knock twice a week instead.

There are seven milk bottles standing on the wall
waiting for the milkman to call,
because he's still doing trade,
been paid rather than getting laid,
and he doesn't have the right skills
to become a greengrocer.

There are six milk bottles standing on the wall
waiting for the milkman to call,
remnants in the bottom turning sour from poverty,

maggots wriggling in defiance
before Mama covers them in table salt
telling me next time to wash the bottles properly
or I'll be put out to pasture with them.

There are five milk bottles standing on the wall
waiting for the milkman to call;
one of the empties was smashed last night
by the delinquent neighbour next-door
who glassed his girlfriend in the leg
after a shocking domestic
because she didn't leave enough milk
in the fridge for him
to turn his cornflakes soggy.

There are four milk bottles standing on the wall
waiting for the milkman to call
and I have to be truthful in admitting
I sipped from one of them,
mouth over cool glass neck,
gulping down creamy nutrition,
wondering why nobody gave me tuition earlier in life
about how good this stuff is when you're hungry,
or thirsty,
or both.

There are three milk bottles standing on the wall
waiting for the milkman to call every second day,
because Mama cut back on the order,
saying I need to drink the free milk at school
dished out to kids like me who get it for free
and I couldn't bring myself to tell her
nobody takes a handout from the classroom crate
unless they want to be bullied outside the school gate
for being poor.

There are two milk bottles standing on the wall
waiting for the milkman to call,

way less than there used to be
since Mama works three jobs a week
and spends her wages down the toon
so she hasn't got time to drink tea anymore.

There is one milk bottle standing on the wall
waiting for the milkman to call;
it's been there for a week collecting rainfall
inside its empty stomach
begging to be taken away to be refilled
so it's no longer famished,
instead of being banished,
cast aside as unwanted rubbish.

There are no milk bottles standing on the wall
waiting for the milkman to call,
because he's not coming around anymore
since they brought in cartons at the supermarket
and relegated him to the dole.

FORK

silver spoon absent
for lower-class lass taking
fork to knife old life

MIME

black
and
white
mime

      plays
      on
      television

           inside
           my
           broken
           mind

                  desperate
                  words
                  echo

                        someone
                        scream
                        for
                        me

BLACKBOARD

Where's my pencil, hey, Teacher?
The writing is on the wall
without one

Where's my eraser, hey, Teacher?
I'm the dinner ticket kid
who has been wiped away
in a cloud of dust
from the blackboard

Where's my book, hey, Teacher?
I'm reading between the lines and finding nothing
but empty space for students
without an affluent background

Where's my ruler, hey, Teacher?
I'm looking for the person in the room
willing to stamp out
perpetuating education elitism

Where's my future, hey, Teacher?
When going to university means
starving on the street and 'being beat'
is not measured in Ivy League grades
but in welts left by the cane down my back

Where's my teacher, hey, Preacher?
Who will take the time to understand
the niche skills it took
to crawl from under the desk
to secure a seat at one

MACK THE KNIFE

Red and white fight with
Sunderland trouble and strife
Ducking Mack the Knife

Black and white vision
Tunnelled football division
No retribution

BOOMBOX

girl from the ghetto
presses play on the
ghetto blaster,
dancing faster,
nothing lacklustre
about the tunes replayed
from Sunday's countdown
from ten to one
getting the lowdown
of the latest chart scene
she just wants to be seen
without the ravine
of rich and poor
where music makes
all things equal
until she stops
to stare at the slot
for the CD she's not got
before pressing rewind
on the top of the pops
playing them again
on the paradox
of the boombox

HAIRSPRAY

Enough hairspray
hardening the fringe of the
nation's northern population

to blowtorch away
any loose ends
from gaslight spite

trying to set us alight
without insight
to the inside of our minds

ANOTHER BRICK

Daddy migrated across the ocean,
Newcastle to Saudi,
to save tax free for an Audi
without serving notice on the repayments
of our ancient junk wheel liability,
leaving no note of departure for the family,
nor a single snap in the album to prove his existence,
nor a single snap in the album to prove mine,
leaving only grief for the living behind
in a child's crushed eggshell mind.

Hey, Teacher,
I need education for survival,
not to be left alone to fend for myself
but to be helped along
to develop a curious mind of my own,
rich with self-control, not thought-control;
don't leave this kid alone
the same as daddy did
when he abandoned the home,
leaving drugs as my only friend
to airbend the mind
into thinking I am worthwhile
and have a place in this dysfunctional life.

Hey, Teacher,
I just learned in the classroom of inclusion
we aren't meant to leave behind
forgotten children who dropped
between the concrete cracks,
hoping moss will grow over them
to hide their ugly existence.

We need to share enough cement to help
each unique person achieve their destiny of becoming

another brick in the wall,
creating diverse new structures in a world
where there is enough space in life's architecture
to rebuild all the broken souls
who manage to clamber over
the barriers of trauma and neglect,
and that anyone who provides a rung on the ladder
is a hero that deserves all our respect.

Hey, Teacher,
thank you for not being circumspect
in changing the curriculum to avoid neglect
of the cowering child in the corner.

IT JUST IS

Our innocent faces were hidden behind
a curtain of dirt from the thick Thatcher air,
streaked with hurt from lack of care,
coal abandoned in the ground,
production ground to a halt,
shipping steel stacked in the yards,
nothing to steal from our broken hearts –
        I'm not proud
        or enraged
        or ashamed …
        it just is.

Electric fire on one bar in the home,
sibling fingers crowded around orange glow
right after bath on a Sunday night,
relieved that the usual Saturday fight
was over between Mama and Step-Papa;
number three or was it four,
we didn't know the man anymore
who made us scrambled eggs on toast
before packing his bags
to coast elsewhere –
        I'm not confused
        or neglected
        or rejected
        much …
        it just is.

A hole in my shoes
as we plod one way across the River Tyne
to lay our hat wherever our home was supposed to be
in the rejuvenated council dumping ground
north of the angel;
she waved at us as we passed her by,
contemporary arms spread wide, larger than life,

ours weary, lugging modern family baggage
heavy with bricks of hope needed to build a new life
in a city rife with a future
carved with a sharp knife
putting deep scars on my wrists
because it was easier
than putting on a smile
with yesterday's socks.
          I'm not messed up
          or put down
          by the people
          who frown down
          their nose …
          it just is.

Crossed the Tyne Bridge again in later years,
marvelling at her green dress which made up
for the absence of green grass accessorising riverbanks,
knowing I would not return
anytime soon to the toon,
but aware I would always see the world
in all her black and white glory,
forever a magpie, born a Geordie,
never resentful of those to the south,
travelling to Shields and beyond from Tynemouth,
          I couldn't care
          who is from where,
          hey, you over there …
          it just is.

Maybe the one with the silver spoon
had a better start than the girl from the toon,
but life is what you make it,
so I don't try and fake it until I make it anymore,
because you might fool them but you can't fool yourself
into thinking it's enough when it not
and you don't want to rot in the bottom of the gutter

with the ones they forgot to fish out,
so I am going to shout just this once
that sometimes it can be unfair
when you're dished more than your fair share
of bad luck leaving you kicked down in the muck
with a mind trying to remind you
                it just is ...
                without
                justice.

HOME COOKED GRATITUDE

Mama cooked today
tinned corned beef mashed with
potatoes and mushy peas –
I licked my plate clean

Put the same clothes on my back
as I wore yesterday
since laundry day is Sunday –
glad to be snug as a bug

Enrolled in new school
where truancy rates are high
and grades are low –
life skills form in the halls when the bell tolls

Mama served my last home-cooked supper tonight
of frozen chips with a Scotch egg
before I boarded the National Express –
full tummy for the one-way trip to my future

AIN'T NO LOVE

INTERVIEW WITH A VAMPIRE GIRL

We were vampires prowling just before dusk
unaware of any underlying lust

Just kids from the block baring our fangs
to attract a replacement for the back of our hands

Seeking the blood of a virgin kiss
to cross it off our to-do-list

Still forming identities, so green and young
I didn't even know how to spell tongue

Yet I remember his name and the softest mess
of lips on mine, an inexperienced caress

Not first crush, first boyfriend, first love, or real McCoy
but first kiss is his, my vampire boy

3AM CINCUAIN

disco
where music plays
lithe bodies freely dance
no past, or future, only now
clubbing

DANCE

movement
unhindered

never felt more free
than when loud music played
shaking off inhibitions

"body and mind peaceful in noise"

DISCO BALL

Saturday night, forget Girl Friday
Cover pain with bright pink lipstick
Punish weary feet in heels
Let life's lost loves slip by
As alter ego
Reflection spins
Underneath
Disco
Ball

FLUORESCENT ADOLESCENT

the
perfect
antidepressant
disco ball iridescent
club fever incessant
dance floor fervescent
neon pink suppressant
yellow band fluorescent
grown up too soon adolescent

AIN'T NO LOVE

City boys preening in their best pressed shirt
Hanging out in defiance in stonewashed jeans
Collar smelling of cheap Old Spice
Breath smelling of pint after pint of Snakebites

City girls parading in their shortest skirts
Toes peeking out from bunion wielding shoes
Bare necks begging for hickey tattoo
Goosebumps defending elements marring skin blue

City love served after last orders called
Pulled on tap down back alley dead ends
A quick fix injection behind abandoned gravestones
Evidence of coupling never embossed on tombstones

City heart beats seven days of the week
Pulsing neon on the Quayside and Big Market streets
Until morning sweepers clean up vomit of self-pity
Ain't no love in the heart of the city

INVISIBLE THREAT

Mama said watch out
for boys taking advantage
of a naïve girl like me
but they came
wearing invisible cloaks

CHARLIE

Grandma introduced me to Charlie,
skipping a motherhood generation
as she handed down that half bottle of spiced scent
packaged in a red box with silver embossed labelling,
dipping me with ylang ylang and prue,
introducing me to adulthood with a hue
fit for a princess.

Basking in Charlie
I mutated from a Prodigy child into a Firestarter
raving in downtown Planet Earth,
my nose so attuned with musky perfume
it didn't notice the smell
of Saturday night on the dance floor,
my body so sensuous it never repelled
the boy at the end of the bar
looking for the garage party plus one.

Charlie says,
"always tell your mummy
before you go off somewhere",
but I didn't listen,
Grandma,
I didn't listen.

THE HOPPINGS

Love was a shared toffee apple
leaving sticky remnants coating teeth
and a discoloured core on a stick.

A hook-the-duck prize
of a goldfish in a litre of water
tied in a clear plastic bag.

Thighs touching on the Waltzer,
bruises worn with pride from the Disco Tagada,
dizziness from a kiss on the American Eggs.

Candy floss sugar rush and foreplay blush,
arm around shoulder on the ghost train,
knowing I'd be ghosted for the second time
when the fair packed up for another year

… and not caring.

BINGO

Eyes down
Did he take my number?
Eyes up

BINGO

HAIR OF THE DOG

We span the two-for-one wheel
in Julie's on a Monday night,
friends getting drunk enough
on anticipation and a one-pound coin
to dance to Jamiroquai
until Tuesday sunrise.

Wednesday was Jesmond
pizza and pasta half-in-half
and a date for dessert
with the Italian waiter
who looked the part.

Being Thursday's child
I had far to go
to travel to the Big Market
by double decker bus
before stumbling
down to the Quayside
for last orders.

Friday night live music bonanza
at Westerhope Excelsior Social Institute
to sip half a lager for fifty pence
with the working men with nothing else
to do, saving our best selves for
Saturday Circus Circus fun
and a Sunday hangover
hair of the dog rerun.

N-TRANCE

love can set you free
when you scan the horizon
to see your first sunrise
without the optical illusion of a mirage
and know the thirst is quenched

YO-YO

I was an up and down yo-yo
wrapped around your finger,
tangled in your string.

You were full of tricks,
The Creeper always checking
if there was someone better
around the corner.

I tried to roll with it
but you wound me up so much
deep down I knew I was always destined
to be nothing more than your toy.

CATPHISH

Ping!
Impromptu connection request
Scrutinise your profile, stranger
Checking for hints of danger
One square jaw
Two turquoise blue, infinity pool eyes
Three is company
Four walls of loneliness keep me online
Five mutual friends in a multi-billion population
Better than six degrees of separation
This is my moment, no hesitation.

Splash!
Good to swim in new social circles
Expand virtual horizons
Tsunami of failed relationships
Left behind stagnant puddles
Fatigued from wading through poses
Of glamourous friends splashed across social media
Desperate not to feel inferior as I soak up images
Voyeurism made legit, nothing to lose
Plunge into exploration with newfound friend
Feet bare of Wellington boots, no raincoat
Drowning in desire, need to acquire
Love to float my boat.

Click!
Unhook safety harness
Allow heart to flutter in the breeze
With the autumn leaves
Tumbling from the branches of brittle trees
Scooped up by the wind
Set adrift, my soul afloat
With ninety-nine red Banksy balloons of hope
Natural instinct following modern romance scent

Zoom in on your snap gallery
Cleft in chin, suntanned skin
Absence of wedding ring makes heart sing.

Like!
Eager acknowledgement back at you
Blue thumbs up … too soon for red love heart
Starry eyes, emoji smile
Onslaughts of LOL and XOXO
Delve into unknown electronic abyss
Suddenly feel decades younger
Navigating unchartered territory
Bated breath, blink, click my mouse
Share my screen, let you into my house.

Chat!
"Hey," you say
Time for a face-to-face match
Bat back witty banter
Long rally of words
Literary prowess game turns into set
Smashes into extra time
Perfect match with no safety net
Umpire a no show, place my bet.
Love
All.

Poke!
Again … again … again
Silence is deafening
Bile of panic rises
Confidence falls
Swipe glass until fingers ache
Likes absent, love hearts cut loose, away on vacation
No posts, or comments, or personal dedication.

Phew!
Direct message

Thankfully we're all good
Your mother unfortunately took ill
Better than finding out you have become sick of me
I'm a terrible person to think this way
Transfer money for her operation
Least I can do
Good Samaritan, add the nought's
Guilty amends for dirty thoughts.

Crash!
Your profile suddenly disappears
Search high and low
Check under every virtual stone
No gateway, bridge, or route(r) taking me back to you
Padlock my heart forever
Time to toss away the key(board)
Impossible to believe I've been phished on your hook
Lock my account, close down love on Facebook.
Block you, block them
The mutual friends
Nothing anyone says can make amends
For this cruel world that was once big
And is now so small
Condensed into the screen
I'm shutting down once and for all.

DIRTY MIND

Washing my hands of you is impossible
Twenty seconds of soap scrubbing
Followed by a dousing of alcoholic sanitiser
Yet still remnants of your skin
Remain under my fingernails
Evidence I once scratched your back

I'm determined to clean up my act
Looking forward and moving into the new norm
Closing my mind to what was and what could have been
Yet still you infect my thoughts
With viral dirt mixed with hurt
Evidence you once stabbed my back

SNAKEBITE

Drinking snakebite pints
while listening to Whitesnake –
reality bites.

JAM AND SPOON

Temporary love –
We jam and spoon right in the night
until dawn breaks.

RAPUNZEL

Beautiful girl
Made fist curl

Locked in tower
Made to cower

Always dark knight
Never white

Drawbridge raised
Alone and fazed

Until time was right
To rise and fight

Leave lair back there
To let down my hair

HOLLOW

Every night you hollowed out my flesh
Horror hidden beneath your costume
Until the light behind the eyes of a pumpkin burned out
And the clock stopped at midnight

ASH

You were the fuel in a fire
forever filled with sparks

The match that held
flame to lust

The combusted relationship
we extinguished with heated words

The one who scorched your brand on my skin
without permission when it was never your property to burn

Leaving nothing but a pile of black ash
marring the surface of a cold hearth

EXPLOSIVE CALAMITY

Four and a half billion years
before our two planets aligned
love was cruel, blind, rarely kind,
then lust became my new fossil fuel
boosting solar system energy for a short while,
gravity forcing sublime rhyme,
a nebula blocking out reality
dust and gas fusing us in explosive calamity,
never contemplating we might need revision,
blinded by illusion encrusted in tunnel vision
not seeing the future eclipse of a lifetime together
when I passed you, you passed me, no more we.

Suddenly we were no longer one earth
where we once rose in synchronisation
in correlation with flirtation,
instead we split apart
and you became my displaced moon
transforming into the singular solar night light
that fought against my sunset plight
as we circled around each other
in a relationship consuming the galaxy
until that asteroid hit
and I was the only person who didn't see the speed
of the collision hurtling towards me –
no more us, no more they, no more we.

The united journey we once embarked upon
has spun undone and become new sun
rising in a new dawn so slow I know
it's time to catch my breath and decompress,
caught up was I in starry undress,
until nothing could prevent the digress
into extinction of a pair of dinosaur carcass
who were never able to commit with conviction

to a home always destined for eviction
as all we ever could be was a temporary addiction
craving you, ravishing me, consuming we.

We now coexist in a galaxy as separate stars
where women are from Venus and men are from Mars,
opposites who met through lust and luck
before grinding to a halt from the mind fuck
of spinning twenty-two Jurassic era hours every day,
cramming in a lifetime of work, rest and play,
morphing into an endless, mindless partnership
where you tried to inhabit my mothership
and I wasn't ready to give in to psychological warfare
knowing we were built on thin air of a wing and a prayer
and I was right to cut loose the disrepair
of lonely heart, needing new start, after we part.

AI

artificial love
blinding my intelligence
until brain kicks in

CALCULATED RISK

It's not clear if we were
an accident waiting to happen
or I was victim of a man-made attack
on humanity

Only you have the means
to fill in the gaps in my truth
but I don't have a gasmask
to protect against your gaslighting

LIT

we went up in smoke
when you lit a fire elsewhere
trying to be lit

NIGHT IN

Dear Tinder,
          all dressed up
          and nowhere to go
          this girl has a date tonight
          with a poem.

APPRECIATED

I'll take what I want and give you what you need,
lust or love, we both need to feed
and feel appreciated,
inebriated, saturated, infatuated,
cause if we aren't intense it makes no sense
to push uphill in self-defence

mode trying to make
our humble abode
work.

So, either you're all in or I'm all out,
peel off my skin, lay down my doubt,
put it to rest when you put me to bed
or the mess we shared
is as good as dead
and I'll go elsewhere instead.

COAT HANGER

Adjust the coat hanger aerial
but it's impossible to tune in
amidst arguments
over television remotes
lost down the side
of the La-Z-Boy
with the forgotten sound
of companionable silence

OUTBREAK

I craved a public
out   break
of our relationship

You wanted to
break   out
in secret with me

As it was backward from the start
the only option was to
break   up

LEV-I

You were timeless denim once
Made of comfortable fabric
A second skin
Moulded to my shape

Over time your love faded
With those old blue jeans
We became washed out
Ripped and full of holes

The attempt to recycle our love failed
In the end you cut our relationship short
Chopped forever at the knees
When you decided to lev-i

RED HAND GANG

foot
in
mouth

your
hands
red

shamed
head
hangs

guilty
cheeks
burn

body
of
evidence

you
can't
dispute

kick
ass
out

my
heart
resolute

never
signed
up

for
trio
membership

red
hand
gang

LOVE IS A BATTLEFIELD

Leave a trail   of   red
lipstick on stranger's collar
in a bloody mess

Prior lessons of
stranger danger forgotten
for another night

Stains from the war paint
left behind on the battlefield
as we search for love

PINK LANE

Dead eyed ladies of the night
Selling their wares on Pink Lane
Opposite central station
Hoping for a train to rain
A pound down on them

Nobody dared judge their tricks
As we headed from
the Tuxedo Princess
In search of the afterparty

We were all in the same boat
Doing our best to stay afloat
Trying to swim across the moat
To a New-castle

BOYS DON'T CRY

I was riddled
with a disease called love
where every day was Friday

You were riddled with guilt
for not loving me back –
We needed The Cure

But it was to wish impossible things –
You didn't need a handkerchief when you left
because big boys don't cry

ROAD

to meet
blind date
ended alone
at my

HOUSE

OMITTED PUNCTUATION

I wanted to be the poem
where you finished my sentences
in places nobody else could fathom

Rhythm which underpinned
the duet in my bed
alongside beat to passionate tango dance

Rhyme giving sublime synchronisation
in a world of polarisation
and reason to return to me each night

Steady stanza giving structure to chaos
amidst surprising impromptu verse
going way beyond simple couplet

Wordsmith of your future with no full stops
only every necessary pregnant pause
between each lustful breath

Omitted punctuation because
we needed no distractions
from the intensity of the moment

So why
did you use a
?

SIMPLE MATH

I once thought my equal
would be the sum of deducting
lies from love and
finding neutral ground

I learned the hard way
my equal is one plus one
never more than two

CUBE (REWIND)

Multiple dimensions formulate the shape of a cube
just as multiple dimensions formulate me.

      This is my

one-sided

      story.

When I was a struggling high school kid,
mean girls used to call me square,
assuming it a flat two-dimensional insult,
but I knew it was the basis on which I
could build a pyramid, or a cube,
or whatever wonder took my mood.

On the surface, flash smile at passers-by,
showing only the angle I want them to see.
People who know me well see my other sides,
loving every corner of who I am.
Others kiss my cheek
with tongue in their own   cheek.
Spreading gossip, ignorant to the fact they are

two-   faced

multiple dimensions formulate the shape of a cube
just as multiple dimensions formulate me.

So, here I am saying I have more than one face,
making me two-faced too.
I'm not too ashamed, cheeks inflamed,
                              to say it.

Every person needs more than two sides
to have any fun when rolling life's dice,
and while socially three is company,
far better to have a fourth wall.
"Hey you… I'm not alone in thinking this,
                                              am I?"

Multiple dimensions formulate the shape of a cube.
How many dimensions formulate you?

Only I can be held responsible
for the shape my life takes,
moving 54 pieces in combinations
through 43.2 quintillion variations
of a Rubik's cube.
Making moves in the right order
to create harmony amidst
                                        chaotic disorder.

For a while you helped me build a fifth side,
adding bricks of confidence cemented with
superficial friends paying social dividends;
an architecturally flawed structure trespassing on the
solid square base of my solitary childhood.
You framed the future as sturdy enough
to keep a roof over my head,
allowing me to call your house
                                        our home.

Until I realised I had a sixth sense,
a waterproof silver lining within the roof,
keeping me dry from storms of lies
muting the sound of incomprehensible cries,
brimming with enough instinct to know
the only love I ever saw,
smelt, tasted, heard and could touch
meant nothing if sixth sense curdled my gut
from the certainty of knowing

you'd put a roof over another's head,
left your tally above their bed,
and I hadn't mis-read the diabolically
                                    dire situation.

You were convinced my cube would cave in
when I made the move to demolish
every brick you ever laid atop my foundations,
collapsing our roof to ground zero.

But I'm still here
with 43.199 quintillion new moves to make.
Now I've removed the toxic side of my life that was you,
and discovered it's easier to think outside a box
with collapsed ceiling
                                      exposing blue sky.

Multiple dimensions formulate the shape of a cube
just as multiple dimensions formulate me.

This is my one-sided story.
I'm not asking you to take sides.

REWIND - Cube was first published in Punch and Judy, by Kelly Van Nelson (Making Magic Happen Press, 2020). The Rubik's Cube metaphor became the catalyst for this retro collection.

HEART

Ain't no love
in the heart of the city
until first discovered
in the heart inside
my own pretty
skin
♥

DON'T LOOK BACK

BIG COUNTRY

No need to wallow in self-pity
Over lack of love in the city

Newcastle my old hometown
Always a hardcore Steeltown

It's a Big Country out there
I found love elsewhere

DECEASED ESTATE

My inheritance will be a debt
owed to the council for backdated rent
for the childhood home that wore a uniform
of roughcast walls and pale blue front doors
decorated in standard government issue paint
to avoid anyone developing an identity complex.

Yet we knew everyone by name
from the ancient inn with beer on tap
to the community centre
with youths loitering around the back
entrance and everyone in between
could sense if you were having a spot of trouble
and would rally round to stand by their own.

Now I have a garden with a white picket fence
and if I pass through the pearlies tomorrow
the wild cats will lick my corpse
until the smell makes someone call for
a housing inspection to clean up the foul mess
and nobody will want to foot the bill,
leaving an inheritance debt owed to the council
for the next generation.

… some things never change.

DON'T PREACH

You knew when you left
what you were leaving behind
and still you didn't look back

Years later I asked why
in what was our last conversation
before you left for the second time

I'm not a baby now, but still
I cry for the words we didn't say,
caught behind the lump in my throat

I hear your voice from heaven
telling me not to be angry,
but Papa don't preach

PLANET EARTH

In the beginning the nausea was constant
As the world span faster than my young years
I yearned for a new beginning
Far away on another planet

My body floated inside the unlucky Apollo machine
Gasping for air, unable to land
For a while I tried to escape
With a little help from my friend   I n t o x i c a t i o n

I lived in that free place
Nestled between reality and surreal
With my feet on the dancefloor
And my head in the stars

I found my inner power in the darkness
Pulsing with the off-kilter beat
Of raw tunes on DJ decks
Generating energy within my soul

Music was my first love
But it won't be my last
For in between the loudest notes
I learned to embrace the peace within me

ACE OF SPADES

played cards close to chest –
dealt myself the ace of spades
to dig bright future.

POP CULTURE

Looking at life through a kaleidoscope
allowing colourful vision and evolving shapes
carte blanche

Philosophy devoid of fixed frame
where the mind is free to roam
in directions unknown to mankind

Music of a new generation
where tomorrow's song
is a free bird

Movie reel of black and white humble beginnings
bursting into rainbow shades in
high definition that can never be defined

Andy Warhol brush strokes crafting
befuddled masterpieces   ↓underground
wrapped in the softest   ↑velvet

Not confined to lower working class
nor restricted to upper stiff lip mass
in that space where anything is possible

EYES IN THE BACK OF MY HEAD

only when I look back
with an open heart
and forgiving mind
can I look forward

BELLYBUTTON OF THE UNDERBELLY

Comfort was living on the underbelly,
relishing in the starkness of darkness
where the neon penetrated with bright stripes of light
and life rhymed during vibrant nights
where my plight was simply survival.

We were teenage dirtbags wanting reality to drift,
with no rift to shift as we passed a spliff
around lips that had never, ever been kissed,
except on a Saturday night
at Bobby's roundhouse underage disco,
or down Felling Bankies pashing alfresco,
until we progressed to pooling together ready cash
to hook a wrap of speed
because each of us delinquents felt the need
to experience brutal impact on the way lungs breathe
next to heart as it raced in whizz pace
to freeze life in the bubble
where stimulants were embraced.

Some of us made it to young adulthood,
while close friends derailed, checked into jail,
and others checked out the cemetery,
pale forever, in their permanent residency.

We were the lucky ones
filled with ten pounds of euphoria,
still alive enough to pop little white Doves,
revelling in ecstasy
because we so desperately
wanted our bodies to be fucked
to forget our minds were screwed up,
raving with strangers in a game of potluck,
spinning around and around
on the revolving dancefloor of the

Tuxedo Princess nightclub,
stuck in a rut with nothing but our gut
instinct to claw us out of the gutter
to see another bird flutter
with the wind beneath its wings.

Discomfort was getting caught like fluff
in the bellybutton of the underbelly,
waiting for someone to pick me out,
clean me up, dust me off
from the hangover permanently adopted
in a place where everything was consumed in excess:
alcohol, drugs, music by INXS;
we all wanted to snort white lines
while listening to Mick cite lines
about us all having wings,
only I didn't know how to use mine to fly
instead of taking a dive –
I had no concept of how high I could actually soar
without uppers in my body as an artificial trapdoor
to escape through.

I got out of there in time
before addiction ruled mine
a life worth ruining,
leaving me on the shelf
to grow old enough to become out of date,
wondering why even addiction
didn't pick to stick with me,
but I don't rate self-pity
or try to pretty up the situation.

I'm still here looking for the sharp edge
in a curved world where intensity
has curled itself around my soul
and I never want to settle for the status quo,
so, I inject myself with enough willpower

to live life by walking on a knife edge of adventure
rather than overdosing on crippling conjecture.

Comfort is still living on the underbelly,
relishing in the starkness of darkness
where the neon penetrates with bright stripes of light
and life rhymes during vibrant nights,
where my plight is not simply survival,
but the revival and new arrival
of every precious moment until death,
hooked to the open mic instead of meth.

STEEL HEART

molten desire
melting logic to liquid -
'steel' my heart away

ALWAYS SPACE

three hundred billion
stars in our solar system –
space exists for you

CATCH MY BREATH

spreading like wildfire
taking the world's breath away –
a virus called love

BORDER CONTROL

borders between us
bodies unable to touch
apart from the heart

FUTURE PROOF

I smile at the colleagues I work with each day
Support young talent in early career
Coach on lessons learned to avoid pitfall repeats
Share words of wisdom on the value of ethics
Put ideas on the table because my voice is a gift
Know when to hold back to let diverse opinions shine
Skills which evolved over many a year
Future proofing my long-term career

I laugh at memories of blue wire busy signals
Telephone cords with more spring than my step
Recall times we spent winding cassette ribbon with pen
To rewind on the minutes of meetings
Lived in an era of binary code
And monitors the size of my fridge
Swopped Nokia for Blackberry
And Blackberry for Apple
Learning the art
Of technology is smart

SHADOW

where I go you go
nowhere to hide away
alone

where you go I go
never abandoned or stranded by my
clone

always there to talk
sense inside my
head

always the voice in my ear
to command taking a chance with my
heart

GEORDIE SHORE

Tennis ball inside old sock slams brick wall
Feet jump elastics, glide over hopscotch
Synchronised chant with Double Dutch skipping
Innocent playground laughter ricochet

Top of the Pops idols rock the TV
Tape mixes recorded to be played back
New Kids on the Block crazy crush head rush
Music was my first love teenage heartache

Saturday job pays for painting the toon red
Bar crawl foreplay to hardcore clubbing
Hands wave in rave to instrumental beat
Stagger home at sunrise for judgement day

One-way ticket to new destination
We disband taking our own separate paths
Ocean waves prevent face to face wine nights
Social media connection maintains our heartbeat

Every decade fate washes the tide in
Four weddings, a funeral, school reunion
Geordie shore rekindled stories are shared
Forever friends time can never demise

THE CURE

Dire Straits after
challenging the Status Quo
and U2 left me

Sting from bad breakups
Led to me finding The Cure
to loving myself

MAKE HAY

hey!
young girl
not a thing
is as it seems
in those distorted
moments of dark despair
when pain slices into skin
staining school corridors bright red
and you're scared the scars won't ever heal
because it's you against cruel heartless world

but the world keeps spinning on its axis
as you discover ways to explore
new avenues paved with kindness
begging resilient steps
towards a bright future
be boldly taken
so your spirit
is set free
making
hay!

lost girl
don't get caught in clutches
of anxious dilemma
it isn't wrong to leave your school
at sweet sixteen
as long as you chase your dream
each day

TEEN ADVICE

each day
as long as you chase your dream
at sweet sixteen
it isn't wrong to leave your school
of anxious dilemma
don't get caught in clutches
lost girl

IMPOSTER SYNDROME

If it were not for the laminated name tag
Stuck to my cubicle with Blu Tack
I would be a nobody

If it were not for burning the midnight oil
Leaving no stone unturned
I would still be barren of business cards

If it were not for practicing debate in the mirror
To remove the quiver in my voice
I would never have influenced an outcome

If it were not for training my brain
To find creative ways to improve the status quo
I would forever be stuck in the way we've always done things

If it were not for building trust
With colleagues who share the load
I would not be able to carry the burden alone

If it were not for doing a good job
In consistently delivering on promises
I would not have a meaningful seat at the table

So it's time to stop doubting myself every day
Pushing to the limit to keep the burning question at bay
Am I good enough?

DETENTION

Hey, Teacher,

I am good enough.
I am good enough.
I am good enough.
I am good enough.
I am good enough.
I am good enough.
I am good enough.
I am good enough.
I am good enough.
I am good enough.
I am good enough.
I am good enough.
I am good enough.
I am good enough.
I am good enough.
I am good enough.
I am good enough.
I am good enough.
I am good enough.
I am good enough.

NEOTERIC DIMENSION (REWIND)

in the mindset of yesterday
grappling with life's demands
living in a parallel universe
each world disconnected from reality
creating a stellar black hole of confusion
causing the blues

in the sphere of a mother
accompanying her daughter at netball
cheering from the sidelines
red cheeks giving away the game
of her disorganised shame
after forgetting the oranges

in the shoes of a leader
motivating teams to reflect on career pathways
they can stroll along
to reach their full potential
recognised by green growth ticks
rewarded by medals of gold

in the ink of a writer
finding the right words
to express what needs to be said
with enough conviction to
tickle readers pink
by turning the rain purple

in the utopia of today
blending every fragment of life
into a melting pot of colourful hope
with no shades of grey clouding the view
to a muse who portrays this neoteric dimension
on a pristine white canvas
with the gusto of painting the town red

REWIND – Neoteric Dimension was first published in 'Broken', by In My View, 2019 (Third Place).

ODE TO RESILIENCE

Resilience,
> you never left thee,
> always present,
> not by my side,
> but inside my mind.

Resilience,
> how art thou
> able to lighten my load
> without ever saying
> a single word out loud?

Resilience,
> you abhor cunning stealth
> of self-doubt rearing head,
> mercilessly chopping it off
> at the gallows.

Resilience,
> resilience,
> wherefore art thou resilience?
> I rouse you today from slumber
> to forever portray my one true love.

RED LIGHT

I want to be your Roxanne,
the lady you turn to in the night,
always burning the red light
of desire, fire
and lustful sin,
without igniting Police chagrin.

I want to be your Roxanne,
always giving more than expected
without running the risk of being rejected,
knowing you feel beyond indebted,
leaving me with way more
than money on my bedside table
because I was never in this game
to abuse a blank cheque book in your name
which goes against this free love
that jointly we proclaim.

I want to be your Roxanne
putting on my best dress,
knowing later you will undress
me back to my bare skin,
exploring the layers
uncovered deep within
my body and soul.

I want to be your Roxanne
who will never be shared
with another boy,
or treat you as a play toy,
in a reciprocal arrangement
of exclusive,
elusive love.

I want to be your Roxanne,
the lady you turn to in the night,

always leaving a red light
burning, certain you'll be returning,
decerning, yearning, always preserving
the Sting in my tail
so hot it can never be derailed or fail
to refill our honey pot,
so sticky it forms a natural clot
of sweet fulfillment.

I want to be your Roxanne,
never walking the streets again
because the streets have no name
and the men have no name
and it's not #metoo, but me and U2,
unveiled and unashamed
in the name of love,
where instead of standing on the corner
I can turn it
to discover a fence of white picket
where I want to build a home
with you …
because even though we are not the same
we are one.

I want to be your Roxanne,
becoming a 'best of' album
instead of a one-hit-wonder
that stems from the classic song
you want to rewind
over and over again,
until you finish my sentence on every replay,
knowing the lyrics to be sung next
will never entertain any other prefix or suffix
and will always be simply
Roxanne.

HOT WHEELS

hot wheels spinning
leaving heart racing
out of control

ROCK PAPER SCISSORS

Trying to find love is
rock paper scissors chance,
some win, some lose,
some find wild romance –
I was just playing the game
for light entertainment.

That serendipity night
I wasn't looking for more
than a goodtime beat, a hit of
murder on club dancefloor,
I was in tune with the tune,
rocking moves so smooth,
caught up in the groove,
I didn't see you moving in with yours.

You bedded me, embedded me,
the jewel in your crown
had me dripping off your arm
while paraded through town;
I didn't care who stared,
I wanted to be there,
all attraction before you
simply couldn't compare.

I was crazy in love, driven scatty, batty,
told that diamonds are forever
just like Shirley Bassey,
till you remixed a
Kanye West conflict stone,
you mined my blood diamond
in Sierra Leone,
still I was blind from the shine
carved from the rough,
such pure caret in us

I thought we couldn't fuck up,
but cracks will always creep into rock.

Trying to find love is
rock paper scissors chance,
some win, some lose,
some find wild romance,
but paper beats rock every time,
apart made no sense
when together we rhymed
and I didn't want to throw it all away.

So legal papers we signed,
wallpapered over the fracture,
painted smile on my face,
faked orgasmic enrapture,
but the superglue couldn't
keep the paper from peeling,
crumbled rock beneath,
I was concealing the reeling.

We tried to keep the
paperchase marriage intact,
but each cut of the scissors
meant the facade of our act
fell in shreds on the floor,
I couldn't take any more,
I lay dead in a heap,
murder on dancefloor encore.

But then you held out your hand
and you polished us off,
gave back shine to our rhyme,
said we'd give it more time,
and here we are still surviving
in this game of chance,
winners amongst losers
in lifelong romance,

where paper beats rock
and rock beats scissors
and somewhere inside rock
the diamond still glitters.

NO PLACE CALLED HOME

little girl
in the dead of the night
head under duvet
listens in fright

    arguments
    screaming
    angry voices
    demeaning

        there's no place called home

big girl
tears; just heard
her father's gone
from cruel world

    anguish
    silent
    mother's hand
    violent

        there's no place called home

teenage girl
crams in studies
distracts mind
from the bullies

    ridicule
    stings
    no relief
    when the bell rings

        there's no place called home

young woman
one-way bus

empty pockets
what's the fuss
    opportunities
    galore
    are what she ran
    for

        there's no place called home

proud woman
now stands tall
faltered
didn't fall

    grass roots
    long dead
    weeds underfoot
    instead

        there's no place called home

TRIBE

loved ones in brood
who make up a home
friends in your circle
ensure never alone
people you meet
create like-minded vibe
wind under wings
make a powerful tribe

SONGBIRD

The first day we met
We were instinctively in tune
A duet with life's chorus in the background
Warm hand on thigh as the saxophone sighed
Songbirds who needed no words to create magic
Rhythmic beat undistracted by noise of the brass band
Sweet music pulsing with the promise of melodic lust
No conductor needed to keep us in sync
A symphony of mutual attraction
We were instinctively in tune
The first day we met

PICK UP STICKS

Pick up sticks,
colourful moments forever transfixed
in eighties canning within tarnished nucleus
of school behind crucifix, red welts
streaked on palm of underage hands,
lifelong angst inflicted from vituperative instrument
that could just as easily have been wielded
by a music teacher to conduct a beautiful symphony
instead of orchestrating a crescendo of pain,
leaving skin inflamed in a trail
of education cremation indignation.

Pick up sticks,
colourful moments forever transfixed
in slow strolls, long distant marathons,
or frantic sprints, grabbing baton with both hands
in the race to be confixed in society,
where I find my place through notoriety
in creativity from embracing
my own form of free-flow poetry,
abolishing ancient rules of traditional verse,
not because I'm born ignorant
or grown up perverse,
but to unleash the power of the letter
in spoken word therapy
where I choose to use metaphor
of wood as my muse
because I should and I could
choose to amuse
myself picking up sticks
in magic box of poetic tricks.

Pick up sticks,
colourful moments forever transfixed,
dropped in a loose bunch on flat table-top,

jumbled in random pile of contacts amok,
facilitating precarious networks to intersect,
criss-crossing through life
until pulled in new directions,
movement inevitable from knock-on effect,
shuffling connections until new bonds form,
while you and I, we stay firm
despite disturbances around us,
never allowing anyone to
extract either party in stealth,
forever touching in an immortal
mental and physical game,
always moved but never moving,
not emotionless, but motionless,
amidst the chaos.

Pick up sticks,
colourful moments forever transfixed
in five-year anniversary of unwavering marriage bricks,
where the roots of family tree
have sprawled deep enough
to enable sturdy trunk to weather thunderstorm,
sprouting new buds of children
that grow into idiosyncratic branches of spawn
as mother nature plays her hand
in making sure we always have
enough trees to replenish timberland,
combatting axe of death from human hand
chopping fuel for fire
causing delicate environment to go haywire,
but still I strive to maintain forest, trees and the wood
of the twigs crackling each day with the roots underfoot.

Pick up sticks,
colourful moments forever transfixed,
a retro game now a poem forever remixed.

COALITION

Maggie at the helm
Future bleak for British men
Coal mines gone to hell

Coal-ition troop
Bury the past underfoot
Labour's Major coup

WALLFLOWER AWAKENING

once a budding wallflower
introvert and invisible
emerging from darkness
deep within earth's core
where once trodden
underfoot

plant solid roots
gulp raindrops to quench thirst
devour nourishment
after years of starvation
turn face to sunlight
relish gift of photosynthesis
develop inner strength
self-cultivating

gain sweet scent of success
stretch after years of hibernation
spread stiff wings
open to embracing the world
petals blossoming
life's new season
rejoiced

wind blows in
shaking the core
ruffling status quo
relinquishing nucleus seeds
scattering ideas
like-minded shrubs
pollinated

procreate colourful talent
flourishing vivid and bold
beautiful garden spawning
diverse and eclectic habitat

sustaining the elements
come rain or shine
blooming

THE EDGE

My feet walk the knife's edge
as in the past I made a pledge
to seek not a new limit
but to discover my already existent
hidden capabilities wedged in my brain
that unless stretched will never reign
or fulfill true potential
leaving me stuck in consequential
thought restriction and sequential
penitential regret.

My ego seeks no affirmation
for lack of humility is damnation
and I found peace in gratitude
for all I am when embracing solitude
inside the comfort of my own skin
where I don't need attestation from him
or her or them or you
to know I'm worthy of being true
to myself and accepting of the knowledge
I am unique so take your critique
elsewhere.

MASTERCHEF

bake me if you like
for the sparse ingredients
in this recipe

there is no icing
or needless sugar-coating
on this concrete cake

WAY BACK WHEN

Way back when glass-bottled milk decorated doorstep
Postie's knock would brighten each day
Bank teller counted coins in the palm of her hand
Ice cream van would serve kids after play

Way back when we drank coffee that came from a jar
Before baristas frothed latte and ground beans
Fish and chips wrapped in newspaper was dinner out
When we managed to budget around meagre means

Way back when lead paint decorated baby's cot
Dormant asbestos insulated roof
Miners oblivious to the perils of black lung disease
In those years before confronting proof

Way back when a typist was sought out for speed
Shorthand a premium skill
When memos didn't come on an email chain
They were written in ink with a quill

Way back when we realised the world had changed
New jobs beginning to pave way
For careers of the future instead of the past
It wasn't just way back when, it's today

A TRIBUTE TO BILLY ELLIOT

Why I prescribe poetry:

Life needs simplicity
Therapy to quash toxicity
Unicorns crave eccentricity

Mind seeks authenticity
Body burns with electricity
Soul consumed with poetry

Side effects:
Image now publicity
Acknowledge complicity

GOODBYE, PET

Working class
Geordie lass

Never wanted to settle
for less than better

Compelled to cross Tyne Bridge
to explore beyond concrete ridge

City tongue craved language and diverse culture
across rolling hills and green agriculture

Time to roll life's dice to place new bet
outside comfort zone, "Auf Wiedersehen, Pet".

PLEASURE DOME

Saturday afternoon at the Spanish City
ride the ghost train to overshadow fear of reality
with trepidation of invading imaginary cemetery
to replace the skeletons in my closet
with the bones of ghouls and bloodshed
and the haunting cries of the living dead
who made me feel on the spearhead
of being alive.

On those remembered days at Whitley Bay
fantasy tried to pave the way
to a better place well away
from all the naysayers
who said local kids had nothing
when we had it all away from home
inside the pleasure dome

until it closed down
leaving nowhere left to clown around
in the ghost town.

Abandoned, decayed, dilapidated,
inside and out deteriorated,
poor, begging with cupped hands
for the neglect to end with mine.

Years slipped by of disrepair,
until injected with a dose of love and care,
slowly rebuilding inner strength,
restoring dignity way beyond former glory
into something iconic where the turbulent history
is what makes her what she is today

… a national treasure.

MUTATE

limitations
with a few carefully
constructed mutations
shake off constricting restrictions
becoming immune from immunisations
of debilitating procrastinations
bringing life changing alterations
and a future filled with
celebrations

DON'T LOOK BACK (REWIND)

We were all born under the same rock
but some were airlifted out
to manicured gardens of posh estates
behind electric gates
with private number plates
in their drives.

The rest of us were abandoned
beneath the shadow of the stone
in the heart of the council drop zone,
everything on loan,
inner-confidence home grown.

Down in the earth with the worms
the tough got tougher
and the rough got rougher –
decapitate the head of a worm
and it regenerates.

Nobody looked back
for fear of seeing
one of the amputated tails,
unable to be revived,
leaving PTSD and guilty tendencies
at being the half that survived.

We were the ones that got away,
living in the present
where a ten pence cigarette
went far, feasting on one puff
before passing on the tar,
and a bottle of Scrumpy was shared with Jack –
we knew how to make fish and bread
feed the five thousand.

Comradery stems from

wriggling together in the dirt
under the turf.

Every kid knew your name –
some used it, others called you worse,
but we all wrapped around each other
when wriggling from the hands of the police.

Eventually we grew into snakes,
shedding our hand-me-down school uniforms
and growing a thick new skin for work,
where we soiled our hands
and coiled our wallets
around the minimum wage.

Even if we wasted the coins on
too much venom on a Friday night
you could always take a loan from your bestie
who never called in the IOU
because it was always paid back
gift wrapped in loyalty.

When the going got tough
we retreated to the clew,
tunnelling deeply in the soil,
churning, yearning for better times.

We were the resourceful generation,
mixing reality with topsoil,
our secretion generating enough
nitrogen for new plants to grow.

Don't look back in anger –
Languor in a place where the
nutrient of life is formed
and the worm is reformed
and transformed.

REWIND - First published in Creatrix by WA Poets Inc. 2021.

THIS IS MY AXIS

I didn't
spin out of control
as a result of your behaviour
but because Mother Earth told me
I was never meant to be
controlled by
anyone

WEATHER GIRLS

For all the girls who held my hand
as I cried over a boy who broke my heart,
or crawled on all fours trying to drown the pain out,
gratefully accepting the tissue from your clutch
to mop mascara streaming down my cheeks –
you are my umbrella.

For all the girls who stood by my side
as I unpicked words spat in anger
and floundered in the pathway to forgiveness,
or choked as I swallowed my pride to apologise –
you are my umbrella.

For all the girls who danced with me
to the tune of music,
celebrating the beat of living in the moment,
relishing being young, free, and stupid,
never judging mistakes,
but helping me avoid
another tangle with a snake –
you are my umbrella.

For all the girls who shared a cocktail
and swallowed a maraschino cherry of a story,
swearing to never break girl code
in a pact you have kept until this day –
you are my umbrella.

For all the girls who know me not
as anything other than a poet on a page,
or the voice trying to mend
a lifelong sore throat
by pulling swollen tonsils out with an open mic
and have been cheering me on from the sidelines –
you are my umbrella.

For all the girls who tilt their faces to the sky
in appreciation of the sun coming after the rain
before turning to the girl on the sideline
reflecting a dose of the light onto them
to assist their growth –
we don't need an umbrella

… we are the weather girls

Hey,
Teacher,
I came back
to visit you,
to stand up front in
assembly hall to speak
words of hope to those lost kids,
with anecdotes of how my books
landed in Academy Award
swag bags on the Hollywood red carpet
and share tips of how to build bricks in the wall.

GROUND ZERO

To my dismay I found the bricks and mortar
razored to ground zero leaving a hole
in my soul where my high school once stood
and no classroom to raise my hand
and ask you questions about
what happened to the girls
like me who wanted
to learn and grow –
what happened,
Teacher,
hey?

L PLATES

Every day I hung my young head
in the school hall
I learned how to find
solace in my own mind

When I drew blood from my teenage arm
in a cry for help
I learned who my lifelong friends were
who never needed to ask why

In those dark moments
after making a bad judgement with a boy
I learned your own company
is better than bad company

Leaving school at sixteen to put food on the table
Instead of earning a certificate of accomplishment meant
I learned the lifelong lesson of knowing I am not worth any less
for the decisions I took to survive

Although it took several attempts
to graduate from my L plates
I learned that having the freedom to go anyplace anytime
is worth fighting for

Three decades passed
trying to make sense of family lost before
I learned that family found
is what truly is important

Picking up a pen
when on the brink
I learned that turning ink into sinking
anxiety in a poem would help me feel reborn

After finding no love in my home city
and crossing the county line to strange lands
I learned the love you carry within yourself
is essential hand luggage while travelling anywhere

TOBY JUG

Anticipation is coming home
to a cold fridge with a door barren
of paintings in bright poster paint
made with miniature hands

Deflation is staring at a mantlepiece of ugly toby jugs
instead of a framed photograph
capturing a shy girl with a gap
between crooked milk teeth

Trepidation is walking onto the stage
for the annual school production
knowing I am solo in having zero
parents in the audience clapping for an encore

Emancipation is the realisation
I am old enough to vote for a democracy
where I have a voice on the other side
of the wall you built to box me in

Cessation is resignation from ongoing oppression
cutting invisible family ties
that bind my scarred wrists
with nothing but infected bloodlines

Condemnation is hanging out the anger to dry
pinning it with splintered wooden pegs
on a washing line with recently cleaned laundry
blowing in the breeze

FEAR

I'm not afraid of dying

I'm afraid of not living
or giving everything
to something promising
in this unforgiving place

or not finding my space
or steady pace
in this race
to chase
a dream

BRIDGE OVER TROUBLED WATER

Papa checked out young.
I was left arguing with Mama,
a bad girl from the North East craving
the bridge over troubled water.

I didn't pray for better days,
I simply knew I couldn't stay,
it was time to move on
and make my own hay
by walking the talk towards
the bridge over troubled water.

Always in the backdrop,
seen from every angle,
I knew this green architectural beast
was no fandangle
and could untangle
the mess I was in if I put
one determined foot
in front of the other and stepped on
the bridge over troubled water.

Mott, Hay and Anderson
designed an icon
decorating Tyneside's horizon,
on the one side sunset and unrest to be left,
on the other a sunrise and previse of the next best
thing since sliced stottie cake from Greggs,
my shoes protected by Blakey's segs
as they scraped deprived pavement in outrage
at having to walk so far to tackle
the bridge over troubled water.

In football, The Magpie's
bitter rivals are The Boro',
but contractor, Dorman Long,
brought talent from Middlesbrough
to the toon when he built the Tyne Bridge

before being cloaked by nationalisation
by British Steel who wanted to
reclaim his international affirmation
for identical work completed
on the Sydney Harbour Bridge
with just a few tweaks to her dimensions
and a way better view
of the opera house instead of Cruddas Park
so those crossing into New South Wales
could see a better head start
than those in Newcastle
trying to keep hope in their heart
as they watched the ambitious depart over
the bridge over troubled water.

In the beginning Newcastle-upon-Tyne
was all that I knew until the wind blew
in new ideas and I had to park all my fears
and shake off the dance trance to take a stance
and grab the chance to advance and enhance
my skills to realise my full potential
outside the council rental on the estate
where I used to skate
on thin ice every day
trying to make my way to
the bridge over troubled water.

In the end I made it to Sydney,
crossing the Tyne Bridge on the way out
and the harbour bridge on the way in,
to join a new community
in the land of opportunity,
but I've never managed to
build up enough immunity to cross
the bridge over troubled water
without being engulfed
in a wave of nostalgia.

DARK SIDE OF THE MOON

I am the bright side of the sun
The dark side of the moon
The sparkle of the stars
With the universe at one

PERSPECTIVE

Looking back I see
everything was meant to be

so I could be free
to become the best version of me

making a difference
in society

ACKNOWLEDGEMENTS

In retrospection, this year just passed has been like no other. With a global pandemic rocking the world, I found myself separated from my husband for months on end, due to lockdown restrictions and border challenges in Australia. As a result, I've had many evenings free to pen the poems of this collection. This manuscript was written in its entirety during the Covid era and working on it has been my silver lining. Thank you, Shaun, for the inadvertent space you gave me to complete another creative project and for what you gave in this window of madness in the name of selfless loyalty to your work commitments, your family back in South Africa, and me and the kids. We will look back on this unexplainable period and know how much love it took to come out the other side.

Kayin, I'm excited beyond words to have you taking a chip off the old block in producing your own poetry, fiction, and film scripts that are finding their own audience. You are way more talented than your old mum! Working on the fusion of poetry and film with you and having our movie reel showcase at the Melbourne Fringe was the best collaboration ever.

Imani, you will always be my sunshine and jelly tots. Thank you for taking me back to eighties hair, lending me your blue eyeshadow, and helping me develop a new glam look to fit with the whole essence of this book. You are a patient superstar for the time you spent taking many photographs that visually capture what I want to express in the quest to make poetry hip again for a new generation of readers.

Karen Mc Dermott. We added another brick! This wall is getting damn tall and the paint keeps getting brighter (A fair amount of vivid cerise this time). You took me to the top of the bestselling charts and kept me grounded along the way, always thinking about what we can cook up next. You taught me how to have fun on this crazy journey, and for a serious workaholic like me, that is truly a gift to be grateful for.

I extend my thanks to Dylan Ingram, the publishing crew at Making Magic Happen Press and all the fellow authors who offer ongoing support and help launch my books with a rocket grenade.

Tommy Woodward, here we go again, with another cover that rocks the shelves. The fine detail you added to the Newcastle skyline depicted on the cover, including the infamous Tyne Bridge, is epic. I didn't even have to brainstorm this one with you! Your conceptual thinking and approach to modern graphic design makes it so easy to work together. You are a super talent with a huge future ahead of you.

Ranfurley (@jp_reuben), thank you for the amazing custom sketched boombox artwork that makes the interior of this book so unique.

To the midnight poets, the slama gangs, the zoom crowd, the MMH Press Poetry open mic regulars, and the whole global poetry community. You are both my pseudo family and my insomnia nemesis, getting me up at the crack of dawn and keeping me there, transfixed on your genius words, while the rest of the world sleeps. Skylar J. Wynter, kudos for coming along on all those 3am business class trips from the outback to Nashville and beyond. A special thanks to all the spoken word event hosts who liked my Nu Shit enough to give me a feature slot and for never judging if I happened to be half asleep and wearing PJ's while performing in the witching hour. Whether virtual or face to face, your friendship means more than you will ever know.

Miriam Hechtman, thanks for refining my novice recording skills to take poetry to our new Wordsmith Poetry Podcast audience and Natascha Moy for putting the dynamic duo together, to Karen Sander for getting me back on the Story Room stage again, and the Generation Women producers for keeping me on speed dial for Team Forties.

Much appreciation also to the booksellers who keep giving me space next to Rupi.

Laura Nisbet, thanks for photobombing my last book into Better Homes Mag and for giving it pride of place on its own special shelf. Hilditch's, we gotta get a retro reunion booked soon. It's been six books since we last almost drowned in the jacuzzi.

West Denton High alumni, our school might be gone forever, but the memories remain. Thank you to all the past students who reconnected and offered support, and to the old friends with the deepest understanding of what it was really like growing up in the ghetto blaster years. I'll pop a Castaway open with you in celebration next time I cross the bridge home.

To my sister, Joanne, I had to reference Bobby's Roundhouse. I followed in your teenage footsteps to dance at the best spots in town. You always had good taste.

As always, Henderson, Doubell, and Van Nelson gangs, thanks for being on the other end of the phone at all hours to talk to a mad poet who is simply trying to make life rhyme every once in a while.

And lastly, to my readers. I am eternally grateful you made it all the way to the end of these epic never-ending acknowledgements. Remember, give Retro to a friend, drop a review, or press rewind on the boombox. Whichever path you take in life, the choice is always yours.

Kelly
xxx

ABOUT THE AUTHOR

Kelly Van Nelson is a contemporary author and poet from Newcastle-upon-Tyne, now living in Sydney, Australia. Her poems, short stories, and articles have featured in numerous international publications and she regularly appears on radio and television discussing current issues prevalent in society. She is represented by The Newman Agency.

Graffiti Lane, her powerful debut poetry collection, showcased at the London Book Fair and became an instant bestseller, raising awareness and influencing change around bullying, mental health, and suicide. *Punch and Judy,* her second #1 bestselling poetry collection, puts the spotlight on domestic violence, generating much needed conversation. She is also the author of Rolling in the Mud, A Short Story Collection, and her books are frequently gifted to Hollywood celebrities, music icons, and Academy Award winners.

Kelly is a KSP First Edition Fellowship recipient, an AusMumpreneur 'Big Idea - Changing the World' Gold Award winner for her creative use of the literary word as an antibullying advocate, a double gold Roar Success Award winner for Best Book (Graffiti Lane) and Most Powerful

Influencer, Social Media Star silver award winner, and bronze winner of the Making A Difference award. She is also a Telstra Business Women's Award and CEO Magazine Managing Director of the Year finalist.

Kelly is the mum of two children, wife of her soulmate of more than two decades, and Managing Director on the executive board of a Fortune 500. In the spare time she doesn't have, you can find her hanging out on the open mic performing poetry around the world. In short, she is a juggler.

www.kellyvannelson.com

www.ingramcontent.com/pod-product-compliance
Lightning Source LLC
Chambersburg PA
CBHW021407290426
44108CB00010B/427